Kenny's Day Off

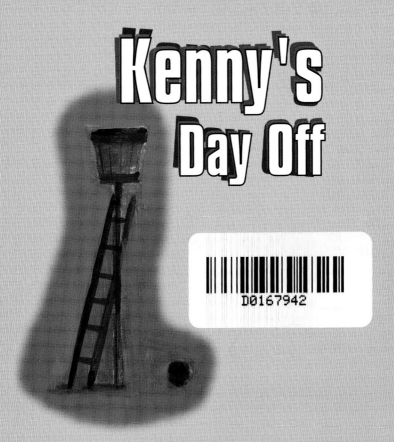

by Babs Bell Hajdusiewicz

illustrated by Larry Johnson

Scott Foresman

Editorial Offices: Glenview, Illinois • New York, New York
Sales Offices: Reading, Massachusetts • Duluth, Georgia
Glenview, Illinois • Carrollton, Texas • Menlo Park, California

"It's not fair!" Kenny grumbled. "Do I really
have to stay here all day? I want to shoot baskets!"

"You know the routine, Kenny," said Mom.
"When someone calls in sick, I have to come in.
I won't leave you at home alone. One day without
basketball isn't going to kill you."

Kenny gritted his teeth.

"I'm sorry," said Mom. "But I can use your help
in the store today. And to thank you, I'll make your
favorite breakfast tomorrow—flapjacks!"

"Okay, I guess," said Kenny. "So people really pay money for this junk?"

"They'll certainly pay more once it's clean," said Mom. "Come on. Let's put some life in this stuff."

"Cleaning won't help," said Kenny grudgingly. "This old lamp must be a million years old!"

"Lighten up, Kenny!" said Mom. "That old lamp actually hung outside a railroad depot in town in the 1800s. Now how about taking these pictures out back and cleaning them? The frames are fragile. So be extra careful."

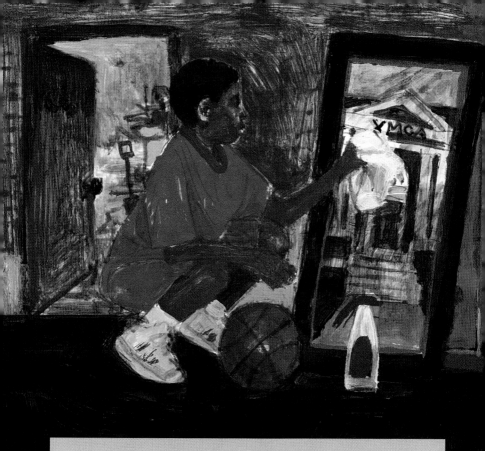

"Some vacation day!" said Kenny as he went outside. "My friends are out playing basketball. And I'm stuck in a junk pile!"

Kenny picked up the dirtier frame and sprayed the glass. "What a funny-looking building," he said as he wiped off a layer of dirt. "It says YMCA. That's where I'd like to be right now—shooting baskets!"

Kenny rubbed harder and the glass shifted in the frame. He felt a gust of air on his arm. He shivered as he looked down at the ground and saw a wrinkled picture of a man.

"Hey!" Kenny laughed. "What's with the weird mustache? And why are you staring at me?"

Kenny felt another gust of air. He shivered again as the picture floated up and away. "Come back here!" Kenny cried.

Kenny scrambled out of the alley and into the street. He snatched the picture.

"Whoa! What's this?" he stammered as he studied the blank paper in his hand. "Where did the picture go? Where's that guy?"

All of a sudden Kenny felt something beside him.
Kenny turned. The man with the mustache stood
right beside him!

"Who are you?" Kenny gasped.

"My name's Earl. What's yours?"

"I'm Kenny."

Kenny heard a thumping sound in the distance.

"Hear that?" said Earl. "Sorry, but I'd better hurry. It's time to play ball."

"Play ball?" Kenny asked. He stared as Earl raced down the street and disappeared behind a building. Kenny gazed at the blank paper in his hand. Then he tossed it in a basket and grabbed his basketball. He ran down the street toward the thumping sound.

"Wait up!" he hollered.

As Kenny approached the building, the
thumping sound grew louder. His heart raced as
he rounded the corner. Then he stopped abruptly.

"It's Earl!" he gasped. "And that's the building
I saw in the picture!"

Confused, Kenny whirled around to look back
toward the antique shop. But there was only an
open field.

In the distance he heard a train rushing along its
tracks. *The railroad depot that Mom mentioned must
be nearby,* he thought.

"See that peach basket up there?" said Earl. Kenny was more interested in the ladder.

"A friend of mine showed me this," said Earl. "Watch how I throw the ball into the basket."

Kenny watched as Earl gripped the sides of the ball and lowered it between his knees. Then Earl tossed the ball into the air. It landed in the basket.

"Do you want to try it?" asked Earl. He scooped the ball from the basket and threw it to Kenny.

"Sure," Kenny said. "I have plenty of time."

Earl gave the ball to Kenny. Kenny placed his hands on the ball and prepared to jump.

"No! Don't jump!" Earl said. "And you're holding it wrong. Here, I'll show you."

Kenny watched Earl toss the ball into the air.

"Like that!" Earl said proudly. "It's your turn."

Kenny grabbed the sides of the ball and lowered it between his knees. He tossed the ball into the air. It landed in the basket.

13

"That was great!" Earl exclaimed. "You're good, Kenny! So what do you think of this new game? Will it put 1891 in the history books?"

"New game? History books? 1891?" Kenny said softly. "I guess so. I bet it will become very popular!"

Earl smiled, "I'd like to see that!"

"Can you do a jump shot?" Kenny asked Earl. "I mean, can you jump and shoot the ball through the basket at the same time?"

"I don't think that's possible," said Earl. "Besides, I don't think anyone would ever want to."

"Well, maybe I'll just try it," Kenny said. He grabbed his ball and carefully placed his hands. Then he jumped higher than he'd ever jumped before! But before he shot the ball, he felt that strange gust of air again. And then he was by himself in the alley behind the shop.

Kenny carefully carried the framed picture inside. "Look what I found, Mom! It's a YMCA! And it says 1891 right here! That's when basketball started! You won't sell this, will you? Please don't, Mom!"

"Well, perhaps not," said Mom. "Hmmm, maybe your day off hasn't been so boring after all! So do you still want those flapjacks for breakfast tomorrow?"